MEDIEVAL KNIGHTS

KENNY ABDO

Fly!
An Imprint of Abdo Zoom
abdobooks.com

abdobooks.com

Published by Abdo Zoom, a division of ABDO, P.O. Box 398166, Minneapolis, Minnesota 55439. Copyright © 2021 by Abdo Consulting Group, Inc. International copyrights reserved in all countries. No part of this book may be reproduced in any form without written permission from the publisher. Fly!™ is a trademark and logo of Abdo Zoom.

Printed in the United States of America, North Mankato, Minnesota.
052020
092020

Photo Credits: AP Images, Everett Collection, Granger Collection, iStock, North Wind Picture Archives, Shutterstock
Production Contributors: Kenny Abdo, Jennie Forsberg, Grace Hansen
Design Contributors: Dorothy Toth, Neil Klinepier, Laura Graphenteen

Library of Congress Control Number: 2019956177

Publisher's Cataloging-in-Publication Data

Names: Abdo, Kenny, author.
Title: Medieval knights / by Kenny Abdo
Description: Minneapolis, Minnesota : Abdo Zoom, 2021 | Series: Ancient warriors | Includes online resources and index.
Identifiers: ISBN 9781098221249 (lib. bdg.) | ISBN 9781098222222 (ebook) | ISBN 9781098222710 (Read-to-Me ebook)
Subjects: LCSH: Knights and knighthood--Juvenile literature. | Civilization, Medieval--Juvenile literature. | Middle Ages--Juvenile literature. | Military art and science--Juvenile literature. | Soldiers--Juvenile literature.
Classification: DDC 909.07--dc23

TABLE OF CONTENTS

MEDIEVAL KNIGHTS

Loyal and brave, medieval knights were warriors who fought for honor. They followed a Code of **Chivalry**.

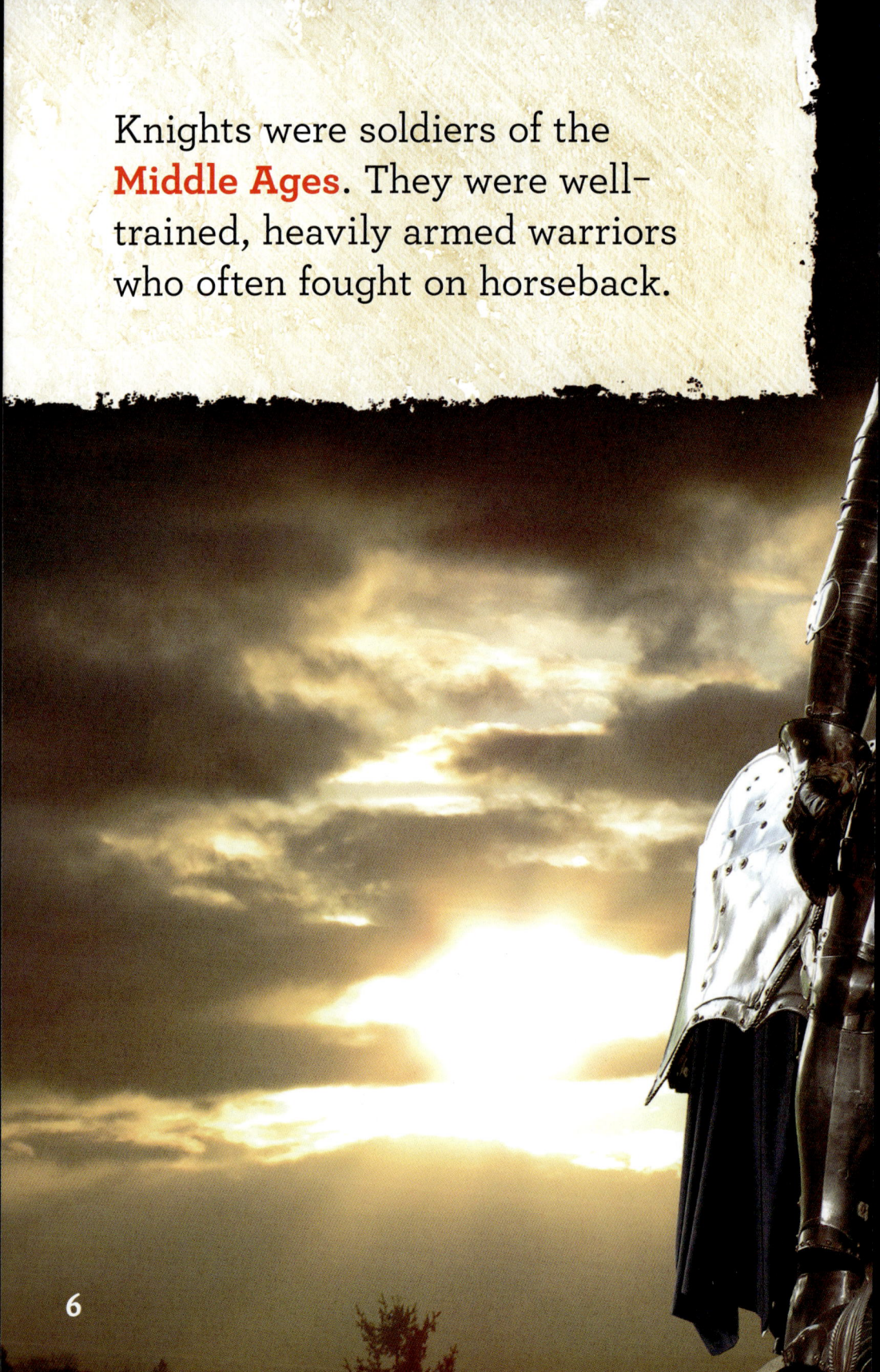

Knights were soldiers of the **Middle Ages**. They were well-trained, heavily armed warriors who often fought on horseback.

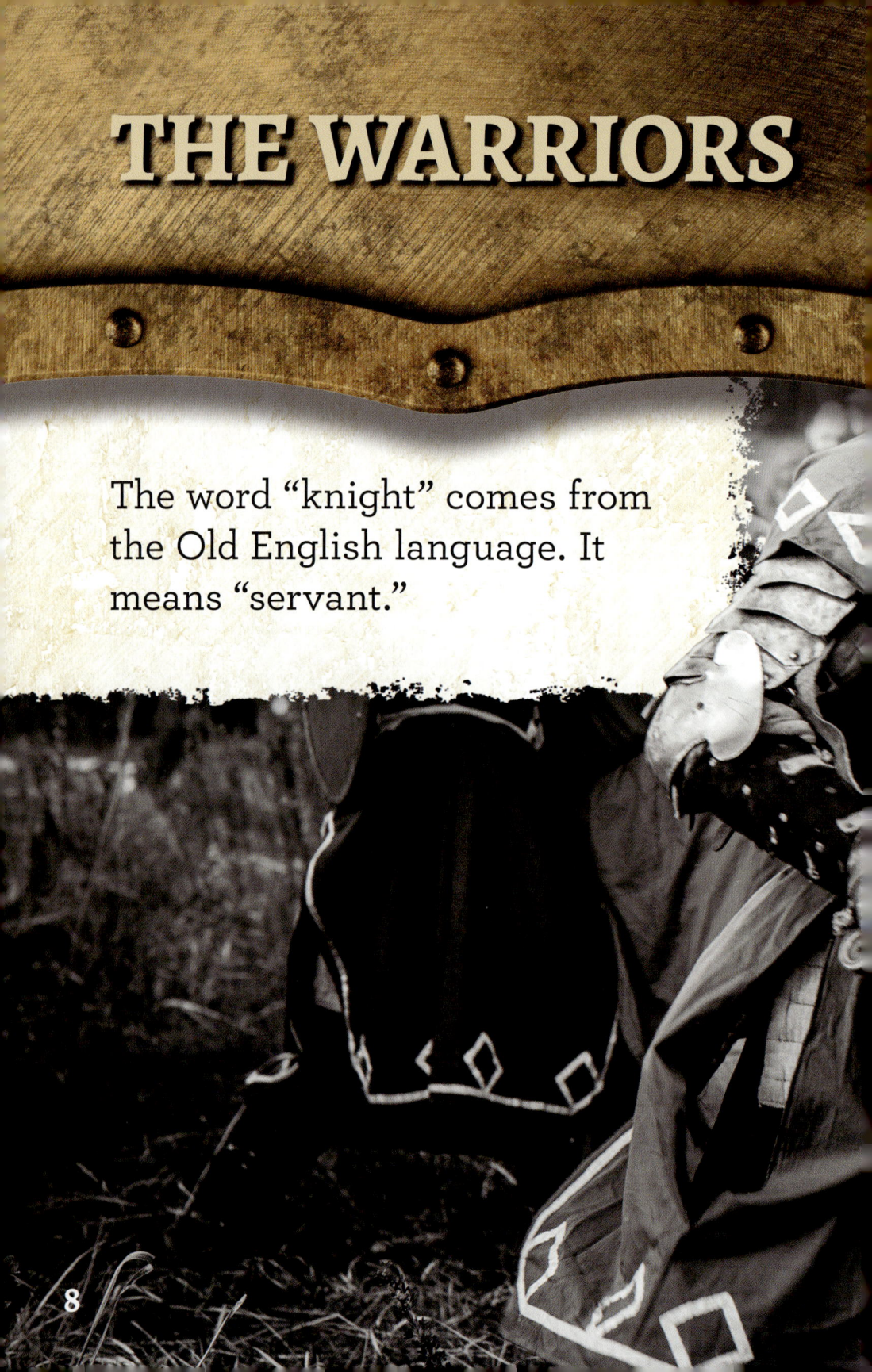

THE WARRIORS

The word "knight" comes from the Old English language. It means "servant."

Knights usually came from wealthy families. To be a knight you needed very expensive armor, weapons, and a powerful warhorse.

Men trained for seven years to become a **page**. It took them another seven years to become a **squire**. Finally, after five more years they would achieve knighthood.

WARFARE & TACTICS

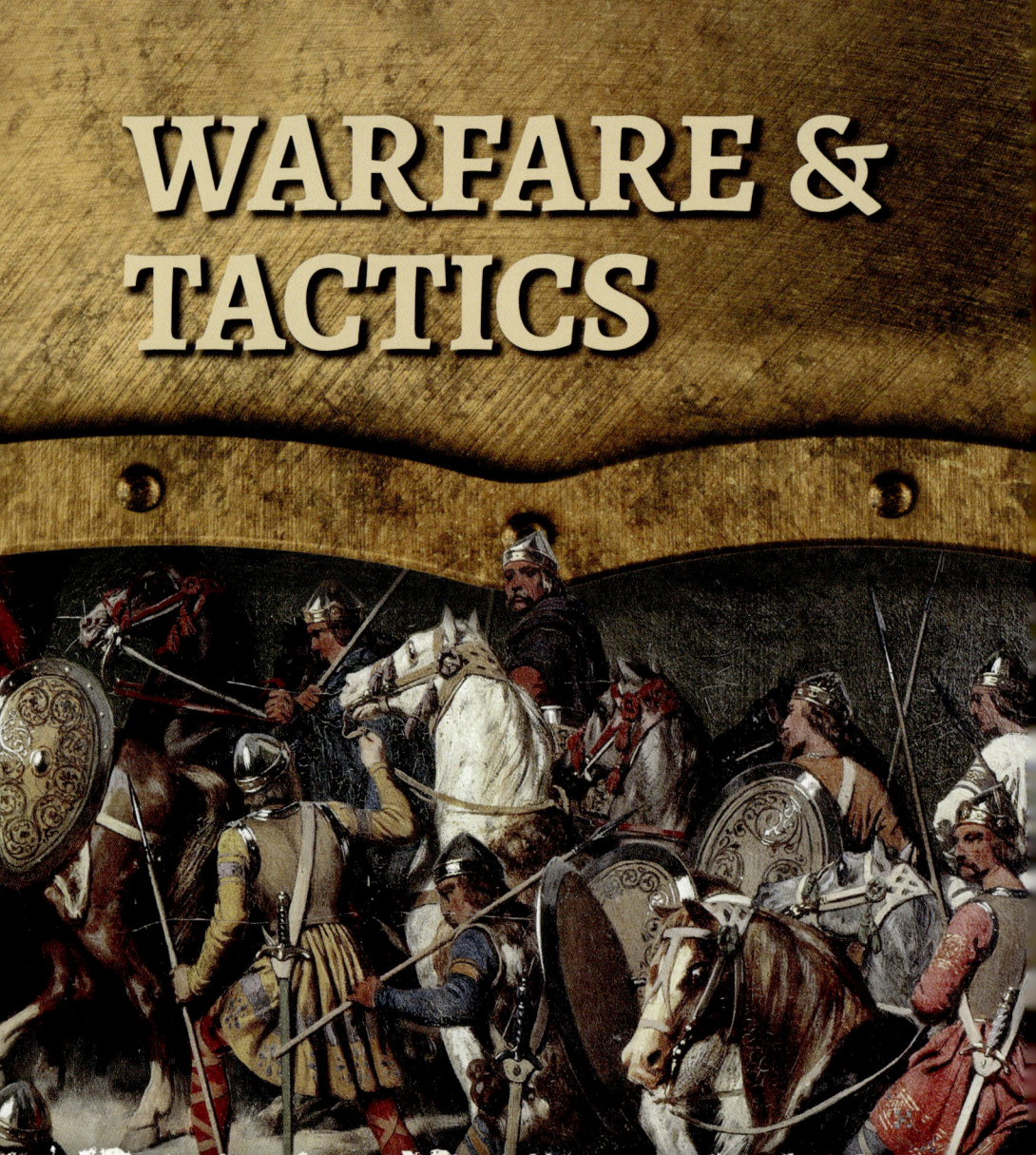

The first knights of the **Middle Ages** fought in the 700s. **Charlemagne** began using soldiers on horseback to fight his battles.

Knights used many different weapons during battle. They used swords, maces, longbows, and **lances** while on horseback.

The knight's warhorse was armored
and trained to kill. These colossal
horses were called destriers. They also
wore armor to protect their necks,
head, and sides.

Knights wore heavy armor made of metal. The two main kinds of armor were chain mail and plate armor. By the 1400s most knights were wearing full plate armor for better protection.

By the end of the **Middle Ages**, knights were no longer an important part of the army. Many countries had formed their own standing armies. And a change in warfare made the heavy armor knights wore useless.

ARE YOU NOT ENTERTAINED?!

Medieval knights have populated mainstream entertainment for decades. Most famously they appeared in *Monty Python and the Holy Grail*.

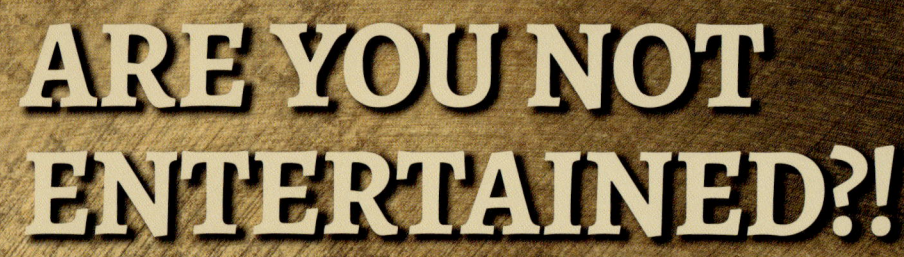

Knighthood is awarded today by kings and queens to people for their achievements. People like Bill Gates, Alfred Hitchcock, and Paul McCartney have received the honor. Only they didn't have to siege castles on horseback.

GLOSSARY

Charlemagne – a medieval emperor who united central and western Europe between 768 and 814 CE.

chivalry – the qualities expected of an ideal knight during the Middle Ages. These included courage, honor, politeness, and being prepared to help those in need.

lance – a long wooden stick with a pointed steel head. Used in battle on horseback.

Middle Ages – the period of European history between ancient time and the Renaissance, from 476 to 1453 CE.

page – helper to a knight. Typically, completing duties like taking messages and organizing armor.

squire – derived from the French words "esquire" and "escuyer" which originally meant "shield bearer."

ONLINE RESOURCES

Booklinks
NONFICTION NETWORK
FREE! ONLINE NONFICTION RESOURCES

To learn more about Medieval Knights, please visit abdobooklinks.com or scan this QR code. These links are routinely monitored and updated to provide the most current information available.

INDEX